RagaMuffin Cats

Kate Conley

**Checkerboard
Library**
An Imprint of Abdo Publishing
abdopublishing.com

abdopublishing.com

Published by Abdo Publishing, a division of ABDO, PO Box 398166, Minneapolis, MN 55439.
Copyright © 2016 by Abdo Consulting Group, Inc. International copyrights reserved in all
countries. No part of this book may be reproduced in any form without written permission from
the publisher. Checkerboard Library™ is a trademark and logo of Abdo Publishing.

Printed in the United States of America, North Mankato, Minnesota.
042015
092015

Cover Photo: Photo by Helmi Flick
Interior Photos: Glow Images pp. 13, 17, 19; Photos by Helmi Flick pp. 5, 7, 15;
    iStockphoto pp. 1, 9, 11, 21

Series Coordinator: Tamara L. Britton
Editors: Megan M. Gunderson, Bridget O'Brien
Art Direction: Neil Klinepier

Library of Congress Cataloging-in-Publication Data

Conley, Kate A., 1977- author.
 Ragamuffin cats / Kate Conley.
    pages cm. -- (Cats. Set 9)
 Includes index.
 ISBN 978-1-62403-813-6
1. Cats--Juvenile literature. 2. Cat breeds--Juvenile literature. I. Title.
 SF445.7.C658 2016
 636.8--dc23
                      2015006609

Contents

Lions, Tigers, and Cats

The sweet, cuddly RagaMuffin is a popular pet cat. Many owners consider the RagaMuffin to be part of their family. But, this **breed** is also a member of a much larger family. This is the family **Felidae**.

The family Felidae includes 37 cat species. Some are wild, such as lions and tigers. They roam forests and savannahs. Others, such as RagaMuffins, are **domesticated**. They make loving pets.

Cats have been domesticated for thousands of years. Ancient Egyptians used cats to help with farm work. The cats hunted rats that were getting into their stored grains. Today, RagaMuffins and other domestic cats provide joy and love to their owners.

RagaMuffin Cats

In the 1960s, a California cat **breeder** named Ann Baker took an interest in her neighbor's cat, Josephine. Josephine had just had kittens. Her kittens were unusually sweet, calm, and friendly. Baker purchased some of the kittens and began to breed them.

From Josephine's kittens, Baker created many breeds. They were called Ragdolls, Miracle Ragdolls, Honey Bears, Doll Babies, Shu Schoos, and Catenoids. Baker referred to all of these cats as Cherubim (CHEHR–uh–bihm). This means "angels."

Breeders and cat owners alike enjoyed the Cherubim breeds and wanted more. But Baker had **strict** rules about breeding. And, she would not let Cherubim be recognized by cat groups.

Baker's **breeders** disliked these harsh rules. In 1993, they formed their own group. They mixed the Cherubim breeds together to create RagaMuffins. People quickly fell in love with the new cats. The **Cat Fanciers' Association** registered the breed in 2003.

The name "RagaMuffin" was a joke at first. It is another term for an urchin. But, the breeders considered their cats to be little urchin cats and the name stuck.

Qualities

RagaMuffins are often compared to teddy bears. They are soft and furry and love to cuddle. Sometimes, RagaMuffins go limp like a ragdoll when they are being cuddled. It is a sign that they are happy.

Unlike many other cat **breeds**, RagaMuffins like to be handled. This makes them good pets in homes with children. It is common to see RagaMuffins patiently sitting in chairs at a child's tea party. They also do not mind being pushed in strollers!

The easygoing RagaMuffin gets along well with other pets. Like a dog, it greets people at the door. But, the RagaMuffin should never go out the door. There are many dangers outside for this **mellow** cat.

RagaMuffins are known as "gentle giants."

Coat and Color

A cuddly RagaMuffin's coat can be medium or long. The fur is soft and silky. The long fur around its neck creates a **ruff**. Its tail is also covered in long fur. The tail's shape is often compared to a bottle brush.

Caring for the RagaMuffin's coat is easy. Despite its length, the fur does not **mat** easily. All the coat requires is a weekly combing. You should use a metal comb made for grooming cats.

A RagaMuffin's coat comes in a variety of colors. It can be white, black, **blue**, red, cream, chocolate, **lilac**, cinnamon, or fawn. Some RagaMuffins are a solid color. Others have patterns such as stripes, spots, or patches that mix several colors.

This RagaMuffin has a tabby pattern. Tabbies are known for their striped bodies.

Size

RagaMuffins are medium to large cats. They reach their full size at age four. Adult males weigh between 12 and 20 pounds (5 and 9 kg). Adult females are smaller. They weigh 8 to 15 pounds (4 to 7 kg).

A RagaMuffin's face is often described as sweet and expressive. It has a short **muzzle**, a rounded chin, and puffy whisker pads. A RagaMuffin's ears are medium sized and rounded at the tips.

A RagaMuffin's body is muscular and sturdy. Its back legs are stronger and slightly longer than its front legs. This allows the RagaMuffin to jump well. Its paws are large and round. There are **tufts** of fur between the toes.

RagaMuffins have large, walnut–shaped eyes, which come in many colors.

Care

A RagaMuffin needs good care to stay happy. Taking your pet to the veterinarian is the best way to make sure it is healthy. The vet will give a cat **vaccines**. He or she can **spay** or **neuter** the cat if it is not going to be **bred**.

Some RagaMuffins have trouble with tooth and gum diseases. It is important to have regular tooth cleanings done at the vet's office. If your RagaMuffin allows it, its teeth should be brushed every day. Cat toothpaste and toothbrushes can make the job easier.

Like other cats, RagaMuffins need food, water, and a bed. They love to play, so they enjoy toys and lots of attention. RagaMuffins also need a **litter box**, which should be cleaned every day.

RagaMuffins enjoy scratching, so make sure you purchase a scratching post. This will keep them from scratching carpeting and furniture.

Feeding

Feeding your pet quality cat food is important. It gives a cat energy so it can play. It also provides **protein**, which keeps a cat's body healthy.

This **breed** has trouble with **obesity**. A vet can recommend how much food your pet should eat. Playful, active RagaMuffins will need more food than those that curl up and cuddle all day.

Some cats are picky about what food they will eat. Dry food is crunchy and hard. Many cats dislike it. They prefer softer foods from cans and pouches. These chewy foods are much closer to what wildcats would eat.

Providing your cat with water is also important. Its water dish should be clean. And, your cat should have fresh water every day.

Your cat's water dish should be left out at all times. That way, the cat can get a drink whenever it needs one.

Kittens

When a female RagaMuffin is about one year old, she can begin to mate. Once a cat has mated, she is **pregnant** for about 65 days. Then she gives birth to her kittens. This is called kittening.

A RagaMuffin mother will have about five kittens in her **litter**. Kittens cannot see or hear for about ten days. They stay close to their mother. She grooms them, keeps them warm, and feeds them.

At first, all kittens eat is their mother's milk. As they grow, they begin to eat solid food. Around this time, they become more curious. The kittens will explore their homes and play with toys. But, they always make sure their mother is nearby.

When a RagaMuffin is born, it is all white. Its color and pattern do not begin to show until it is older.

Buying a Kitten

It is important for kittens to stay with their mother when they are young. She cares for them and teaches them how to groom themselves. Kittens are old enough to leave their mother when they are between three and four months old. They can then be adopted.

Is a RagaMuffin the right cat for your family? If so, look for a responsible **breeder**. Good breeders will know the health background of their cats. The kitten will also have had all of its **vaccines**.

At its new home, your pet needs a few things. A kitten loves to play, so toys are important. Lots of play can make a kitten tired. It needs a soft, warm bed for naps. Water and food should also be available. These items will make a RagaMuffin happy in its new home!

A RagaMuffin can be a loving family member for 12 to 16 years.

Glossary

blue - a coat color that is bluish gray.

breed - a group of animals sharing the same ancestors and appearance. A breeder is a person who raises animals. Raising animals is often called breeding them.

Cat Fanciers' Association - a group that sets the standards for judging all breeds of cats.

domesticated - adapted to life with humans.

Felidae (FEHL-uh-dee) - the scientific Latin name for the cat family. Members of this family are called felids. They include lions, tigers, leopards, jaguars, cougars, wildcats, lynx, cheetahs, and domestic cats.

lilac - a coat color that is pinkish gray.

litter - all of the kittens born at one time to a mother cat.

litter box - a box filled with cat litter, which is similar to sand. Cats use litter boxes to bury their waste.

mat - to form into a tangled mass.

mellow - pleasant and agreeable.

muzzle - an animal's nose and jaws.

neuter (NOO-tuhr) - to remove a male animal's reproductive glands.

obesity - the condition of having too much body fat.

pregnant - having one or more babies growing within the body.

protein - a substance which provides energy to the body and serves as a major class of foods for animals. Foods high in protein include cheese, eggs, fish, meat, and milk.

ruff - long hair that grows on the neck of an animal.

spay - to remove a female animal's reproductive organs.

strict - following or demanding others to follow rules or regulations in a rigid, exact manner.

tuft - a small bunch of hairs that grow together.

vaccine (vak-SEEN) - a shot given to prevent illness or disease.

Websites

To learn more about Cats,
visit **booklinks.abdopublishing.com**. These links are routinely monitored and updated to provide the most current information available.

Index